HOW TO WIN POLITICAL ELECTIONS

*Strategies for Planning,
Establishing and Running
Successful Political Campaigns
in Africa*

DR CHARLES OMOLE

TABLE OF CONTENTS

INTRODUCTION

"In democracy, every election is a learning process. You learn from every election, the one that you win and the one that you lose" declared the famed Indian politician Salman Khurshid. But there is no way you can learn from every election if there are no systems and methods in place to guide the process. These methods and processes that guides the art of campaigning will be the focus of this book.

The suitability of candidates is not within the scope of this book. Those are moral and ethical judgements that are outside my intent for this work. So, any candidate, whatever their political bend can use the principles in this book. But as will be made clear later as you read on, having a message that is beneficial to the majority of people will only help a campaign gain acceptance and support from the electorate. Assuming there is a fair electoral system in place, winning political elections anywhere in the world has two basic components. First relates to factors that are within the control of the candidate, while the other are factors outside of the control of the candidate.

This book relates to the factors that are within the control of the candidate. These are the technical elements of electioneering and campaign management. From setting up campaign operations, to managing the press to crafting your message and dealing with the electorates; all these are discussed in this book.

The second component relates to factors outside the control of the candidate and these cannot be fully addressed by any one book. In fact, some believe these are so volatile factors that they are impossible to predict outcomes. And when you then introduce the African context; the outcome becomes volatility on steroid.

This relates to the unwritten and fluid world of politicking and deal-making. From wining the hearts and mind of party elders and officials, managing and relating with salient stakeholders in the party, obtaining essential backings from giants within the party to managing the balance of power within the party and so on.

These are factors that a candidate cannot fully control and require such a bespoke range of strategies that one size cannot fit all circumstances. A political strategist will be needed to help craft responses and plans based on prevailing circumstances at every stage of the electioneering campaign. This is particularly needed during the intra party primaries stage.

Once a political party adopts a candidate as the flag bearer, the inter-party campaign with the opposition is a lot more amenable to systems, structures and processes that will be discussed in this book.

Election campaigns in Africa are still littered with accusations of corruption and vote rigging such that some believe a systemised campaigning model is impossible in the continent. This has indeed been the case for many decades especially with the interjections of the military in governance in many countries.

Others have had little opportunity to experience democracy with the sit-tight dictatorial leadership in place for many decades. But with the global attitudinal changes against military coups, there are less and less of it taking place in Africa these days.

Additionally, with the introduction of more electronic-aided voting system by more and more countries in Africa, a need has arisen for a systemised and methodical approach to campaigning as mass rigging of elections are now more difficult that previously.

If an electoral system allows for easy rigging and manipulation, then there is no book that can effectively cover all the intricacies of that. So, I must make it clear that this book will be most useful in African societies where there are reasonable and fair electoral systems in place.

An incumbent government that is bent on rigging an election will throw away the rule book and do whatever it feels are necessary to win. No manual can be written to reflect the multifaceted atrocities that tend to follow such deviation from democratic norms. Therefore, it is my assumption that there is a reasonable (I know no institution is perfect) and independent electoral body in place in any African country that will use this book. I am writing this book to help political parties, strategists and politician across the continent build effective campaign machinery to support their political ambitions. Gradually going into history are the days of haphazard, disjointed campaigning in Africa.

With an overwhelming youthful population and its consequential surge in the use of social media and mobile technologies, African politicians cannot afford campaigns that lack zest and focus. This is now the time to build systemic, orderly, innovative, research-based and engaging political campaigns.

Over the last thirty years, I have been a part of many political campaigns across Africa as a strategist and consultant. My job required me to know a lot about the personal circumstances of the candidates in order to devise a strategy for them; hence utmost discretion was always needed.

These non-disclosure agreements I have signed over the decades mean I really cannot give too much specific references to campaign exercises as both the countries and candidate may become known by the discerning readers. So, I have kept the book neutral and focused on tasks and exercises to help the reader design and construct a formidable campaign.

The book is not meant to give an impression of a one size fits all approach to political campaigning but to discuss only general principles that guides successful campaigns. Different countries will need to apply different rules and strategies to reflect the various jurisdictional framework across Africa.

There are situations that will not be suited to generalised prescriptions and only the keen and knowledgeable eyes of a political strategist will be required. Such esoteric situations may not get relieve from this book, but I hope the reader will at least know how to search for a solution.

To be concise; this book assumes the candidate has decided to run for a political office. And all he/she needs is how to go about setting up the campaign infrastructure. Therefore, the book starts in Chapter one with how to conduct the initial start-up research to inform the direction of the campaign.

I have designed this book as a project manual rather than an academic textbook. I have included different Exercises and Appendices to make the book more interactive and practical. And to be honest, I have also excluded certain elements as it is not my intention in this book to give a complete A-Z of building and running a political campaign on the cheap.

For instance, I have removed a whole section on strategies to incentify¹ voters from this book. Magicians do not reveal all their secrets to the general public. Voter incentives come in different forms. In Nigeria for example, it is crudely referred to as "Stomach Infrastructure".

But there are plenty of ways to legitimately encourage specific catchments of voters to vote for your candidate. However, I will not be diving into that in this book as the recommendations will need to be bespoke to each country and different socio-cultural esotericism. My aim is to give enough details to demonstrate what can be done if you apply yourself innovatively. I will then hope the services of a strategist will be engaged to help fill in the blanks. The steps and strategies discussed in this book will apply to all political campaign at any level from local to

---

¹ This is an external reward system that is put in place to encourage action

national campaigns. The scope of some activities will therefore need to be adapted to suit the specific campaign type.

A successful political campaign is not necessarily one that leads to victory in the poll. You can have a successful campaign and not win the election. Success or otherwise of a campaign is determined by the goals set for it in the first place. Politics is a game of strategy.

People contest elections for various reasons, knowing they cannot win. Some contest elections to position themselves strategically for political appointments; others contest to become more known by the electorates preparatory to a future election in a few years. So, a successful campaign is one that meets or exceeds the goal or goals set for it. And as the agreed goal or objective of the campaign will only be known to the inner caucus of the campaign; only a candidate can say if his/her campaign has been successful.

The strategy for getting elected may involve contesting in multiple unsuccessful elections. Such roadmap will be part of a comprehensive political vision. This book is therefore a technical book on how to establish a viable campaign for any political office at any level in Africa.

Finally, this book does not deal with the art of politicking in itself. That is a more complex undertaking as there are countless permutations and responses. Running a professional campaign alone may not get you elected without the art of politicking being mastered by the politicians. But the best politician with unquestionable politicking skills will struggle to get elected without a professional and effective campaign machinery behind him. Hence, this book will be indispensable to politicians or strategists planning to be part of a campaign anywhere in Africa.

I have deliberately not touched on the issue of manifesto production in this book. As this book is aimed at campaigns at all levels, the importance of manifesto in local government election is not as much as in national elections. Parties across Africa do not have the ideological clarity to create the usual Left–Right political divide common in the developed democracies. So, it is assumed that the political party manifesto already exists to be able to utilise the strategies in this book. The message of the campaign discussed in here will be a reflection of the manifesto.

I hope this book will enable you to ask the right questions and raise the right issues if you plan to be part of a political campaign. More importantly I hope it shows you the need to engage a strategist to help steer your campaign to victory. Happy reading and wishing you all the best.

Dr Charles Omole
2017

CHAPTER ONE

INITIAL START-UP RESEARCH

So, a candidate has decided to run for a political office, what happens next? At the earliest stage possible, an initial research need to be conducted to assess what will be needed to make a success of the campaign.

There is need to conduct an initial wide-ranging research before an election campaign can be put together. This research should ideally take place before a candidate declares his/her candidacy. This is because some of the outcomes of the research will determine when and how the candidate declares publicly.

A declaration made in a posh hotel in the capital city may have a different impact compared to that made in the slum with supportive crowd around the candidate. It is all about messaging and we will look at this later. But the initial start-up research must cover certain key areas and subjects. The key subjects are as follows:

The Election Rules

First, we must determine the type of election in which the candidate will be running and what will be the rules of the election. Much of the basic strategy depends on this information.

- This Campaign is for an executive/legislative office?
- We need a majority of the votes to win.

- Is there possibility for a run-off election or is it 50% plus 1?

You should definitely research the laws and, if they are complicated, you may want to ask a political lawyer to draft a memo outlining the most important points. Missing a deadline or violating some part of the law could end your campaign before it has even begun

The Constituencies

Once you have determined the basic election rules, you should start to gather as much information on the constituencies and the voters as possible.

- How large is the constituency in which you will be running?
- What type of terrain will you have to cover as you campaign?
- What type of transportation will you and the supporters need to use?

- How has the population of the constituencies changed since the last election?

You need to analyse the political landscape in which you will be operating.

- Who are the important political players in the constituency and party?
- How strong are the various political parties?
- Who are the civic and business leaders that can influence the campaign?

Winning the support of a particularly influential leader or traditional chiefs in the community can often make the campaign much easier, especially in rural communities where many still defer to community and traditional leaders for guidance.

You also must understand how voters get their information.

- What are the local media outlets in the constituencies?
- Who are the reporters and what are their deadlines?
- How will the election be covered and how does the press view the various candidates and parties?
- How is the ownership structure and political leanings of the press/media in the area?

To develop a comprehensive press strategy, it is important to have as much information on the media as possible.

The Voters

You will need to break the voters in the constituencies into manageable groups. This is the basis you will later use to develop a strategy for targeting particular voters. The following are some of the questions you may want to consider.

- Is there a voter file/register or accurate list of all possible voters available to the campaign?

- What support is there for various political parties?

- What is the demographic composition of the voters?

- For example, what are the income levels, education levels, professions, religious backgrounds, age, gender, etc.?

- Where do people work, shop and play?

- What is the geographic break down of the voters?

- What percentage or how many people live in the city, in the rural areas or in small villages?

- How would you describe your supporters and those voters you hope to persuade?

Voters with similar characteristics may have similar interests and may tend to vote the same way. Seniors will be less interested in schools and more interested in pensions while young mothers will be more interested in schools and less interested in pensions.

By determining how many senior citizens there are and how many young mothers there are, you will be better able to target your message to groups that matter to your success.

The Coming Election

Next, you should look at the factors that will affect this next election, namely the various issues that concern voters and other political campaigns, which are being waged in the State.

- What local, regional or national issues are important to voters?
- What will motivate voters to go to the polls?

- How would you describe the voter mood?
- Which other elections will be on the same day?
- Will candidates in these other races help or hurt your campaign?
- Is there the opportunity to work with other campaigns in a coordinated manner?
- What effect will other campaigns have on the election?
- The candidate's relationship with his/her party and other candidates on the same ticket will affect your strategy.
- Your campaign's message should complement, or at least not contradict, the other messages.

The Candidate

The most important factor in the next election will be the candidate. During your strategic planning session, you need to honestly and candidly judge the strengths and weaknesses of your candidate.

As you do this exercise, you should also look at your candidate from the point of view of your opponent. What you may view as a fresh new face with new ideas, your opponent may view as a lack of experience.

You may want to organize your assessment into various sections, such as the candidate's childhood, education, work history, immediate family, and past appointments etc.

It is important to look for both strengths and weaknesses in all of these areas. By finding weaknesses early, the campaign will be better prepared to deal with them and respond to charges that may come up later in the campaign.

Too many candidates have lost because they refused to deal with past mistakes and were caught off guard when their opponents painted the picture of their mistakes in a very unflattering light. Controlling the narrative is very important. And in today's fast paced media climate; the person that speaks first can easily have the loudest voice.

The Opposition

Once you have determined your own candidate's strengths and weaknesses, the next logical step is to repeat the process for your opponents.

If you are facing several opponents, you should determine which are your strongest competitors for the loyalty of voters you hope to attract. Again, you can organize your assessment into various sections and look for both strengths and weaknesses.

Your opponents will not be forthcoming with information about themselves. You will probably need to do some digging to find reasons for voters to vote against them and for your candidate.

Too often candidates and campaigns view opposition research as looking for the one scandal that will finish off their opponent's campaign. This may happen, but more often what we find is patterns of behaviour that you can use to persuade voters to either vote against your opponent or for you.

You will use this to create a contrast between your candidate and campaign and your opponents' campaign when you develop your message, but this process is the basis for finding that contrast.

The other mistake campaigns often make, is saying that they do not want to wage a negative campaign. Researching your opponent and waging a negative campaign are two entirely different things.

By not taking the time and doing the hard work of opposition research, you forfeit the ability to be prepared for what your opponent will say and do and to build the contrast between yourself and your opponent.

As you gather your opposition research, you must be extremely well organised: list the sources of your documentation, and have a system in place that will allow you to quickly access the information. It will do no good to know something and not be able to provide backup of the information.

All of this research should be gathered together in a binder for easy referral and referenced for easy tracking. Being meticulous and organized now will save a lot of time and energy later.

CHAPTER TWO

SET YOUR CAMPAIGN GOALS AND OBJECTIVES

You need to set objectives for what your campaign need to achieve genuinely. It is not every campaign that leads to an election victory. You must be realistic about your goals. There are candidates that know that to win an election in two election cycles ahead; they need to start contesting for political posts now.

Even though they may not be able to win currently; to them, a successful election campaign will make their names more familiar to the electorates, in ways that can be leveraged in future elections.

So, a successful election campaign is not only that which result in victory. You can have a successful political campaign despite not winning. Success of a political campaign is determined by the realistic object set at the beginning. These goals are usually not made public; but the campaign inner circle must know what their reasonable expected outcomes should be.

In setting campaign goals and objectives there are several parameters that need to be considered. Some of the factors (not an exhaustive list) commonly taken into account are:

- What is the total population of the state
- What is the total number of voters
- What is the expected turnout

- How many votes are needed to win
- How many households do these voters live in

The ultimate goal of almost every political campaign is to win elected office. What you need to focus on is how to determine what must be done to achieve that victory.

A political election is a game of numbers. Too often campaigns forget to calculate how many votes will be needed to guarantee victory and determining where these votes will come from. They then spend their precious resources of time, money and people trying to talk to the whole population instead of the much fewer voters they will need to win.

The strategy of a campaign is to reduce the number of voters with whom you need to communicate aggressively to a much more manageable size. As part of your research, you should determine the total population of the constituencies, the total number of voters, the expected votes cast, the number of votes needed to win and the number of households in which these voters live.

"Total population" is all the people who live in your target constituencies. Considering children too young to vote and people not registered to vote, this number should be larger than the total number of voters.

"Total number of voters" is all the voters in the target constituencies who are eligible to vote and can possibly vote in a given election.

"Expected turnout" is the expected votes cast in an election. Not every voter will vote. Often, we can determine how many voters will vote by looking at past elections. But this may be an art rather than a science for many nations in Africa. If there was 35% turn out in the last election and there are no added factors this time to change the situation, you might figure that about 35% would vote in the

same election this time. But this is not a certain prediction.

This is a very speculative number. What we are looking for is the total number of votes needed to guarantee victory in the race. If you need a majority of the votes to win, this could be 50% of turnout plus one vote.

In many cases you only need a plurality of the votes cast or more votes for your candidate than any other candidate in the race receives. It is important to convert this percentage to a real number. How many actual votes will guarantee your victory?

Setting a Campaign Objective

Using your research information and best judgment, you need to answer the following questions and incorporate the answers into your written Campaign Plan:

1. How many people (not just voters) live in the State?

2. How many of these people are able to vote in this next election?

3. What percentage of these voters do you expect to vote in the next election?

4. How many expected voters is this in real numbers?

5. How many candidates will be running for this position in the primaries?

6. How many of these candidates could be considered serious?

7. If the primaries election were held today, what percentage of the vote do you think each candidate would receive?

8. What percentage of the votes cast will be needed to win?

9. How many votes cast in real numbers are needed to win?

10. If you talk to ten average voters, how many can you persuade to vote for you as at today?

Setting a campaign objective and goals is essential. This will determine what success looks like for the campaign. This objective should only be known to the inner circle of the campaign.

Success may not mean winning the election. It all depends on your objective. A candidate may just want better name recognition as a way of positioning himself for the next election in a few years. For such a candidate, winning is not the intent of the campaign.

Setting a realistic campaign objective is therefore the first pivotal decision any candidate need to make.

CHAPTER THREE

TARGETTING THE VOTERS

Once you decide how many votes you need to win and, therefore how many voters you need to persuade to support your candidate, you need to determine what makes these voters different from other voters who will not support your candidate.

This process is called *"targeting the voters"* or simply *"targeting."* The point of targeting is to determine which subsets of the voting population are most likely to be responsive to your candidate and focusing your campaign efforts on these groups of voters. Your media strategy and channels for instance will be determined by your target audience.

Wise Spending

Targeting is important for two reasons. First, you want to conserve those precious campaign resources of time, money and people, and secondly, you want to develop a message that will best persuade those voters you still need to convince to vote for you.

Suppose, for example, that you decide that you need to communicate with 33% of the voters to win. If you could identify exactly which voters were most likely to deliver that 33%, then your campaign could reach them with one-third of the resources that you would need for an untargeted campaign.

Put another way, if your campaign had the resources to reach every voter in the constituencies one time, you could instead target your efforts to reach your most likely supporters three times.

Candidates that do not take the time to target their voters will waste scarce campaign resources on people that will never give their vote. A part of targeting voters is to look for voters who have emotional reasons to vote for your candidate. For instance, language, tribal, ethnic, religion, education and other affiliations to create kindred connection with the candidate.

You need to determine who the best audience for that message will be. This will help you determine what you can say that is likely to persuade them.

An important rule to remember is that as a party or candidate tries to reach a broader and broader audience, then that party's or candidate's message becomes defused and weaker for each part of that audience. Ultimately, the party or candidate that promises everything to everybody has an empty message that no voter will find credible or compelling.

The goal of targeting therefore, should be to focus your campaign effort on a range of voters that can deliver approximately the same number of votes that you set as your campaign goal as explained in the previous Chapter.

If your target audience is too narrow, you will not attract enough votes to win. If your target audience is too broad, your message will become diffused and candidates with better focus will steal parts of the message - and the electorate - from you.

Targeting and persuading voters
Generally speaking, there are three types of voters:

- Your supporters
- Your opponents' supporters and

- The Undecided (those voters in the middle who have yet to make up their minds).

Your supporters are those who have already decided to vote for you. Your opponents' supporters are those who have already decided to vote for your opponents. Those voters in the middle who have not yet decided and still need to be persuaded to vote for one or the other candidates are called persuadable voters.

It is some portion of these persuadable voters whom you want to target and with whom you want to communicate your message. Remember that a political campaign is a communication process.

In politics, communication is vitally important because perception is everything. Reality is not as important as what the voters perceive as reality. So, you must communicate in ways that cuts through the fog of disinformation and fake news out there. If you lose the communication battle, you will lose the electoral war. Thus, attention and resources must be given to ensure a smooth and efficient communication strategy is in place.

Once you have determined that you need to persuade only about half of the electorate or less to vote for your candidate, you need to figure out what makes your potential voters different from the others. There are two ways to determine this.
These are:

- Geographic targeting and
- Demographic targeting.

Most campaigns will use some combination of both methods.

Geographic targeting
Geographic targeting is simply determining who will vote for your candidate based on where they live. For example, let us say that

candidate "A" lives in town "A" and is well known and liked by his neighbours. Candidate "B" lives in town "B" and is well known and liked by his neighbours. Most of candidate "A's" supporters are going to come from town "A" and he needs to go to town "C" to persuade those residents who are not already committed to a candidate in the race that he is the best candidate.

He would be unwise and wasting his time to go to town "B" and try to persuade those residents and neighbours of candidate "B" to vote for him. Kindred affiliations tend to create emotional pull that sometimes become irrational. People can sometimes still vote for their own even if they know he is not the best candidate.

Demographic targeting

Demographic targeting is splitting the voting population into various groups or subsets of the population. These groups can be based on age, gender, income, level of education, occupation, tribes, language or any other distinct grouping. The point of breaking the population down like this is that similar people are likely to have similar concerns and vote for the same candidate.

Often when determining which groups will be persuaded to vote for a candidate, you should look for groups to which the candidate belongs. Say the candidate is a 38-year-old, educated, small businessman, married with a son and a daughter in school, living in the largest city in the State.

His target groups are going to be young people between the ages of 25 and 40, small business people, and parents with school age children. He is less likely to appeal to groups of the voting population to which he does not belong.

If you sell your candidate as the best to appeal to most demographics, then he/she need only to communicate a persuadable message throughout the campaign to win.

There are two things that can make this targeting less likely to work. First, the demographic groups you choose are too small. Second, there are other candidates with similar backgrounds who are appealing to the same group.

In both cases, if another candidate is also appealing to this same group or it is not a large enough part of the population to provide the margin of victory, then the campaign needs to look to collateral groups or those groups nearest in interests for further support.

In the above example, he may want to expand his message to include people with a higher education (usually professionals).

He would want to broaden his message to appeal to teachers and doctors, which may work nicely with his message to parents with school age children.

The point of all of this is to do the math and figure out how many voters in a particular group can be expected to vote for the candidate if they hear a message that addresses their concerns.

You shouldn't expect to win 100% of the vote of any population but if, with a little effort, you can expect to receive 6 or 7 out of every 10 votes cast, then this is a group of voters with whom you should be in touch and target comprehensively.

You will not be able to come up with very precise numbers for these groups (politics, after all, is an art, not a science). However, going through this exercise and determining numbers for your subsets and cross-sets will help you determine whether your targeting strategy is realistic or not.

An important part of demographic targeting is determining which demographic groups will not be part of your targeted audience. During your strategic planning session, you should, for example, state explicitly *"we will not target government workers"* or *"we will not target young entrepreneurs."* This exercise will help you avoid the trap of defining too wide a targeted audience.

It is often easy to determine which demographic groups you are willing to give to your opponents once you have decided which groups are ours. They are the opposite of the groups that you consider to be your best target groups.

Problems with Targeting

Again, demographic targeting is not a precise science; even in the best of circumstances, definitions of demographic subsets are fuzzy and overlap with one another. They can be made more difficult by three factors:

1. A large number of candidates in each race, which forces candidates to consider groups from which they will receive much less than half the vote.

2. The lack of available, accurate demographic data in many African countries. This will pose some challenge for candidates in many nations on the continent.

3. The undeveloped self-identification of individuals as having specific interests based on their demographic characteristics.

The data collection business in Africa is still at an infant stage. So, a lot of segregated data does not exist at least not in a reliable format. A candidate may need to commission its own research into obtaining some of these information as part of his political campaign.

This could be a differentiation factor compared to the opposition and allow his communicate more effectively than his opponents. Nevertheless, it is important to do this exercise and look at these issues.

Incentives for Voters

Like I stated in my Introduction to this book; I will not be exploring this subject in this book as that will be giving away too many "trade secrets" so to speak. There are many ways to incentify voters in different cultures and socio-political environments across Africa. So, there cannot be a one size fits all approach. Hence the specifics need to be first explored before a package of voter incentives can be put together to fit the needs of a campaign.

There are many political strategists out there that can help with this. My team are also available to help get this done in any country in the continent. There will always be legitimate incentives to get voters support in any culture. Knowing what to do for each target audience is the strategy that must be got right.

EXERCISE 1

ACTION CHART/WORKSHEET

	Likely Voter	Potential Voter	Non-Voter
Likely Supporter	A Solidify Support Base	D Focus on Motivating to Vote	G Possible motivation effort (last priority)
Potential Supporter	B Primary focus for message communication and persuasion	E Secondary focus for persuasion	H No Program
Unlikely to Support	C Possible Communication (low priority)	F No Program	I No Program

Box A: People who are most likely to vote and are most likely to support you are your base of support. You should, first of all, plan activities to solidify this support.

Box B: Likely voters who are potential supporters are your number one target for your persuasion efforts. Spare no effort on these voters.

Box C: Do not spend too much time on people who aren't likely to support you. In fact, your activities may make it more likely that they will go to the polls and vote for your opponents.

Box D: Likely supporters who are only potential voters must be persuaded to vote. Target these people with motivational messages and a strong Election Day push to make sure as many of them as possible vote.

Box E: Potential voters and supporters are important but not crucial. You should focus on them only after you have communicated with Boxes A and B.

Box G: Possible target for motivational efforts. But do not spend scarce campaign resources here until you have thoroughly covered the boxes above or if you need these votes to win. Your time, money and people could be better spent above.

Boxes F, H, and I: Do not waste efforts on these voters.

CHAPTER FOUR

VOTER ANALYSIS AND UNDERSTANDING TARGET AUDIENCE

Having determined a target audience for your campaign, you should make an effort to understand the members of this target audience thoroughly.

The more understanding you have of the target audience, the better your capacity to reach them and get their support. The four areas you should analyse are values, attitudes, issues and desire for leadership qualities.

Understanding your Audience

There has to be some basis to understand the needs of the target audience. The key factors are:

VALUES

What are the core values that unite the voters in your target audience? For example, which do they value more: Social protection or economic opportunity? Societal order or personal freedom? Stability or reform? Peace or security? What values do they share with the rest of the population? What values set them apart from the rest of the population?

ATTITUDES

Are voters optimistic or pessimistic about the future? Are they trustful or mistrustful of government and other social institutions? Do they feel better off or worse off now than in the past? Do they want change or stability?

These are just some of the questions to consider.

ISSUES

What are the important issues that will make voters sit up and take notice of this election? Generally, you should know whether voters are more concerned about economic issues, social issues, or foreign policy issues.

Examples of more specific questions to ask might include the following: Is controlling crime more important or less important than it was in the past? Will your position on education investment be important in this election, or will no one care?

LEADERSHIP QUALITIES

What qualities do voters most want to see in their leaders? Are they looking for stable, experienced leadership, or do they want someone young and dynamic who will shake up the establishment? Would they prefer leaders from the established political class, or do they want leaders who can relate to the concerns of the common man? The key here is to understand what the voters are seeking in order to either sell yourself as the most suitable candidate or try to change their mind through strategic differentiation.

Strategic differentiation is when a candidate knowing he does not fit the parameters voters are seeking for but still trumpets his own suitability through difference. In the USA for example, when Ronald Reagan was running against Walter Mondale in 1984 presidential elections.

An issue for many voters was the age of Reagan compared to Mondale. Many considered Reagan (at 73) as too old and wanted a younger candidate. But at the television debate, Reagan confronted the age issue through strategic differentiation by turning a liability into an asset.

"I will not make age an issue of this campaign. I am not going to exploit, for political purposes, my opponent's youth and inexperience,"[2] Ronald Reagan quipped during the 1984 presidential debates when asked if, at 73, he is too old to be President.

Suddenly, the voters' quest for youth was compared with experience that comes with age. That response during the debate changed many minds in America. The Republican actor-turned-statesman ended up winning by a landslide. That is an example of classic strategic differentiation.

SOCIOLOGICAL RESEARCH

Whenever possible, your voter targeting and analysis should be tested through solid sociological research. Campaigns that are not based on solid research are like drivers at night without headlights. They often do not

---

[2]http://content.time.com/time/specials/packages/article/0,28804,1844704
_1844706_1844612,00.html

see what is right in front of them until it is too late.

Most politicians everywhere believe that they have a natural gift for understanding "the people." They believe that they know, without doing research, what issues to discuss, what values to invoke, and what concerns to address in order to attract the interest of their voters. They are often surprised either by the results of a political poll or by the results on Election Day.

CHAPTER FIVE

DEVELOPING YOUR CAMPAIGN MESSAGE

Once you have decided who your target audience is, you need to decide what you will say to persuade them to vote for you. This is your campaign message. It tells the voters why you are running for this particular office and why they should choose you over your opponents for the same office. Sounds simple, doesn't it? Well, once again, it is deceptively complicated.

For example, let us start off by saying what a message is not. A campaign message is not the candidate's program of what they will do if elected. It is not a list of the issues the candidate will address and it is not a simple, catchy phrase or slogan.

All of these things can be part of a campaign message, depending on whether or not they will persuade voters, but they should not be confused with the message. A Campaign message is a simple statement that will be repeated over and over throughout the campaign to persuade your target voters

What voters care about and how they get their information
In political strategy, there are two important things you need to remember about voters. The first is what is important to them and the second is their sources of information.

Take a minute to think, what are the most important issues in the average voters' minds? Their list of priorities is probably something like the following:

1. How are they getting along with their husband, wife, boyfriend, girlfriend or whatever?
2. How are their children or parents doing, either in school or in life?
3. How are they doing in their jobs or whether or not they will have enough money to get by?
4. How is their football team is doing, why do they keep losing and whether or not they will be able to see the next game?
5. Who should they vote for in the next election?

The point is that you and your election campaign are pretty low in the average voter's list of priorities and rightly so.

All of the other things higher on the list will have much more direct impact on their lives in the very short term and, with a little attention from them, they will have much more impact on those things.

The second thing to remember is that voters are being bombarded with information every day. They get news on television and the radio, they get reports at work, they get advertisements all the time, and they hear that juicy piece of gossip about the neighbour down the street.

Candidates think that their competition is the other person running for the same office, when in reality their competition for the voter's attention is all the other sources of information the voter receives every day. Your campaign message has to break through that thick wall of other information.

So, while candidates and campaign workers are spending hours and hours, days and days, months and months, thinking about, worrying about, doing something about this campaign, voters will give you a minute or two of their precious time and attention. You must not waste it.

Advertising companies understand all this. That is why they come up with a clear, concise message and spend a lot of money making sure their target audience sees, hears and tastes that message as many times as possible. You must do the same thing. You can spend hours and hours writing the most thoughtful position papers and newsletter articles, but if the voters throw them away in 15 seconds, if no one reads them, you are wasting your time.

Characteristics of a good message
- A message must be short
- A message must be truthful and credible
- A message must be persuasive and important to voters
- A message must show contrast

- A message must be clear and speak to the heart
- A message must be targeted
- A message must be repeated again and again

A message must be short

Voters have very little patience for listening to long-winded politicians. If you cannot effectively deliver your message to a voter in less than one minute, then you will surely lose that voter's attention and probably their vote.

A message must be truthful and credible

The message needs to come from the values, practices, policies and history of the candidate. It cannot be inconsistent with the candidate's background. In addition, your message should be believable; candidates who make unrealistic promises simply add to voter apathy. Voters must believe what you say, both about yourself and what you will do, is true.

It is therefore critically important to back up your statements with evidence of experience or knowledge from your personal past. Saying you understand a problem or issue without demonstrating why or how you understand it, is a waste of your time and the voters' time.

A message must be persuasive and important to voters

You must talk about topics that are important to your target audience. These topics will often be problems that voters face every day in their lives, not issues that politicians think are important to public policy.

Voters are more likely to support candidates that talk to them about their jobs, the children's education or their pension then a candidate that talks about the budget, even though the budget may deal with all of these things. Remember you are trying to convince the voter that you are the best candidate to represent them and persuade them to do something, namely vote for you.

A message must show contrast

Voters must make a choice between you and other candidates. You need to make it clear to the voters how you are different from the other candidates in the race by contrasting yourself with them.

If every candidate stands for economic development and national security, then voters will have no way of making a clear choice. If, on the other hand, you support tax cuts for this particular industry and your opponents do not, then the voters will have a very clear choice.

Filling out the message box, which will be discussed in some detail later, will help with developing a clear contrast. Appendix One also provides some advice on how to draw a clear contrast with your opponent.

A message must be clear and speak to the heart

Your message must be delivered in language the voters use and understand easily. Too often politicians want to impress the voters with how smart they are, using technical words that either the voters do not understand or have no real meaning for them. You do not want to make the voting public have to work to understand what you are talking about.

Creating a visual image in the minds of voters is much better. Talk about people, things and real-life situations to describe abstract ideas, such as "economic policy."

Politics is an emotional business and politicians who appeal to the hearts of voters generally defeat those who appeal to their heads. This does not mean that you should abandon the intellectual basis of you party or candidacy or that you should underestimate the intelligence of the voter. This means that you must find a way to tie your campaign message to the core values of your voters and make it clear that you understand the problems they face every day.

A message must be targeted

As discussed in the previous chapter on "Targeting the Voters", if your campaign message speaks to everyone, then in reality, it speaks to no one. The people who will vote for you are different from those who will not vote for you and both groups have different concerns.

Your campaign must determine what these differences are and address your message to your likely supporters. In many cases, voters just need clear information about who really represents their interests. If they have that information, they will vote for that person. Politicians often fail to provide that clear information. They seem to expect voters to either somehow know it without being told or wade through everything the politician says to figure it out.

A message must be repeated again and again

Once your campaign determines what message will persuade your target voters to vote for your candidate, then you must repeat that same message at every opportunity.

Voters are not paying attention to your campaign. Just because you say something does not mean they are listening or will remember what you said. For your message to register with the voters, they have to hear the same message many times in many different ways.

So, if you change your message, you are only confusing the voters. And you must remember the first rule of political communication. This states that: You have not communicated until you have been understood. Speaking or releasing a press statement does not mean you have communicated. You must also be understood by the target audience.

EXERCISE 2

1. **Make a list of all the reasons why voters should vote for your candidate or your party.**

- Now, choosing the most compelling reasons from above, write a brief statement about your candidate. This should be the answer to the question *"why are you running for this office?"* or *"why should I support you?"*

- Now, read the statement aloud and time yourself. You must be able to complete the statement in less than one minute. If you go over a minute, you must trim your message.

- Takeout any long phrases or explanations. Remember that voters will not be paying attention to all of your ten-minute speech.

Grade your message against the above criteria.

1. Is it credible and truthful?
2. Do you backup your statements with personal experience from your past?
3. Are you talking about things that will be important to your target voters?
4. If you are running over one minute, then there are probably a lot of useless words and phrases that you can delete.
5. Do you offer a clear choice between your candidate and your major opponents?

Now rewrite your statement, taking into account those things you missed the first time. You still must keep your message under one minute. As you write and rewrite this statement, as you begin using it as you talk to voters, it will continue to improve.

EXERCISE 3

The aim of this exercise is to help the campaign craft a focused message. Additional details about this is included in one of the appendices.

The American political strategist Paul Tully designed the following exercise to help candidates design their messages and think through their election strategies methodically and thoroughly.

He called this exercise the *"message box."* The message box requires candidates not only to determine what they will be saying during the campaign, but also how they will respond to their opponents' attacks.

⚆ On a large piece of paper draw the following graph:

What We Say About Us	What We Say About Them
What They Say About Us	What They Say About Them

⚆ Now fill in each box with as much information as possible.

WHAT WE SAY ABOUT US

How do the candidate and the campaign define themselves? This quadrant is filled with all the positive things the campaign wants the voters to know about your candidate.

WHAT WE SAY ABOUT THEM

How does your campaign define your various opponents? This quadrant is filled with all the negative things the campaign would want the voters to think about your opponents, the reasons why voters should not vote for them.

You may not say these things directly, but you should at least know what they are.

WHAT THEY SAY ABOUT US

In this quadrant, the campaign must begin to view your candidate and campaign from the point of view of your major opponents.

What would the opponents want the voters to think about your candidate and why, in their opinion, should the voters not vote for your candidate?

WHAT THEY SAY ABOUT THEM

As you continue to view your campaign through the eyes of your major opponents, now look at how they would define themselves. Why, in your opponents' opinion, should voters vote for them?

If done correctly, the complete message box should outline everything that could possibly be said during the election campaign by both your candidate and all of your major opponents. This includes things that may go unsaid or charges made by implication.

For example, if you say that you are the more experienced candidate, by implication you are saying your opponents lack experience. By saying you are honest, you can imply that your opponents are corrupt.

Your opponents can do this to your candidate as well. If, for example, when they say that they care about education, they are implying that you do not care about education. How will you respond to their charges, both stated and implied?

Often the difficulty is putting yourself in the role of your opponents and view your opponents positively and yourself negatively. Remember, just because your opponents say it does not mean that it has to be true. The real question is what will voters believe? If you do not respond to what they say, the voters may take their information as the truth.

The other important part of this exercise is to have answers for the possible charges your opponents will say about you. If they attack you or blame you for something in one of their boxes, how do you respond in your boxes?

CHAPTER SIX

RAISING CREDIBILITY WHILE BUILDING VOTERS FOLLOWERSHIP

As you consider your message and develop the contrast with your opponents, you should keep in mind that what you want to accomplish in the end is to have more credibility with your target voters than you opponents have. In other words, you want more of your target voters to view you as the better candidate and vote for you.

There are usually two ways to accomplish this.

First, you can do and say things to *raise your credibility* in the eyes of the voters. You may do this by concentrating on your positive characteristics and popular stands on issues.

Second, you can try to *lower your opponents' credibility* in the eyes of the voters. You may do this by pointing out what voters will view as the negative characteristics of your opponents or unpopular positions on issues.

Which of these methods you choose and in what combination most often depends on what position you find yourself in over the course of the campaign. Often, if you are ahead in the polls and can expect to win easily, then you can concentrate on raising your credibility.

You will not want to mention your opponents and bring attention to them. You also do not want to risk alienating voters by running what may be viewed as a negative campaign or unnecessarily attacking your opponents.

On the other hand, if you find yourself behind in the polls, raising your credibility may not be enough to win.

In this case you may want to raise your credibility and, at the same time, work to lower your opponents' credibility. In a sense, you have nothing to lose (you are already losing) by attacking your opponents and everything to gain (you may win).

Perfecting the Campaign message

You may think of your campaign's message as the trunk of a large oak tree, strong, stable and well rooted in your candidate's values and personal experience.

Following this analogy, the campaign issues that you will discuss are the tree branches, covering a wide area but all firmly connected to your message tree trunk.

Similarly, your campaign must cover a broad range of issues that concern your target audience. However, in order to address these issues effectively, in order to avoid confusing your target voters with a jumble of incoherent program ideas, you must tie all of your issues to your campaign message

The Buhari/Goodluck Campaign in Nigeria in 2015 is a good example of messaging. After sixteen plus years of the same political party in power (PDP); and with the economic stagnation and recession looming, the Nigerian people were ready for change. So the Buhari campaign's simple message was clear: *Change or more of the same.*

Every campaign activity stayed on this same message. So much so that every Nigerian knew the Buhari campaign for its change mantra. The fact that the details of what that change represented was not fully understood is another matter.

The Buhari campaign did an excellent job of tying each campaign issue to this message of change.

It should be noted that the Buhari message strategy met all of the criteria for a good message. The campaign message was based on good research. Political polls and focus groups showed that the Nigerian people were, in fact, hungry for change.

The message was short, reliable and credible, important to a majority of voters, and it showed contrast with incumbent Goodluck and the PDP, and spoke clearly to the heart of the people.

Candidate Buhari stayed on message continuously. He repeated the same message of change at every opportunity.

Selecting Campaign Issues
It is important not to confuse a problem with an issue. A problem is a condition that needs

addressing, such as economic problems. An issue is a solution or partial solution to a problem, such as increased investment in education and small business to address problems with the economy.

As you consider what issues your campaign will address through its message, there are two important things to remember. First, how important is this particular issue to your target voters? Second, which candidate has the better position on this issue in the eyes of the voters?

Too often, candidates either focus on issues that are not important to voters, ignoring more important issues, or they focus on issues where their opponents' can claim with a certain amount of credibility or a better position on the issue.

EXERCISE 4

DETERMINING ISSUE IMPORTANCE AND POSITION

Suppose that your candidate is considering ten issues that may become factors in the upcoming election campaign. In order to preserve the focus of your campaign, you want to concentrate on only two or three, but which ones? Using this type of graph may help you choose.

First, rank the ten issues (A through J) in order of importance to your target voters (the numbers along the side of the table). In this example, Issue C is most important to voters, followed by Issues G, F, J, E, A, D, H, B, and I respectively.

Second, rank the issues in order of how well your candidate does on these issues in comparison to your major opponents (the numbers along the right side of the box). In this example, the voters believe the candidate will best be able to address issue G, followed by Issues J, A, I, B, E, H, F, C and D respectively.

Issues	Importance	Position
A	5	8
B	2	6
C	10	2
D	4	1
E	6	5
F	8	3
G	9	10
H	3	4
I	1	7
J	7	9

Now, plot out these ten issues as shown on the graph below, placing them in the various quadrants. The example should look something like the following graph:

Very Important/Poor Position					Very Important/Good Position				
10	C								
9								G	
8		F							
7							J		
6				E					
5							A		
4	D								
3			H						
2					B				
1					I				
0	1	2	3	4	5	6	7	8	9	10
	Less Important/Poor Position					Less Important/Good Position			

Your campaign should focus on the issues that fall into the upper-right-hand quadrant

Stay on message

Once you have developed a clear, concise, persuadable message it is important that you use that message at every opportunity and not deviate from it throughout the campaign. This is called "staying on message."

By using the same message in all your voter contact, you are less likely to confuse voters who may not be paying close attention and reinforce what they have heard. It is often said that voters have to hear the same message as many as seven times for it to sink in and register with them.

Often the opposition or the press will do something or say something that will drag you and the campaign "off message." If you respond, you will not be talking about the issues you want to talk about but will be talking about the issues your opponent wants to talk about.

In most cases, you should respond to any charges but then quickly shift the conversation back to the issues and the message you want to address.

CHAPTER SEVEN

DEVELOPING A VOTERS CONTACT PLAN AND STRATEGY

Once you have decided whom you will be talking to and what you will be saying, the next step is to decide how you will be saying it. In other words, how will you get your campaign's message out to voters?

First is the rule of finite resources, which means that you must determine how much each method will cost in terms of time, money and people.

Second is the interchangeability of the resources and the methods, meaning that you can often accomplish the same task using different resources.

Finally, there is the effectiveness of each method at persuading voters, identifying supporters and turning out your vote. It is important to plan well in advance for each phase of the campaign, including turning voters out on Election Day.

In developing a contact plan, some key considerations are:

- The rule of finite resources
- Interchangeability of resources and methods
- Effectiveness of your voter contact
  - Persuade target voters
  - Get out the vote
  - Voter identification
- Types of voter contact activities

o Literature drop
o Literature handouts

The rule of finite resources

As stated before, a political campaign is a communication process and all campaigns have three basic resources available to accomplish this communication - time, money and people.

Every decision to do something is a decision not to do something else. You want to make the largest impact on the voters while using as few of these resources as possible.

Interchangeability of resources and methods

Suppose you decide that you need to persuade 10,000 voters to vote for you. One thousand reliable volunteers can go door to door tomorrow and persuade 10 voters each to vote for your candidacy (no time, no money but lots of people). By yourself, you can personally talk to 10,000 voters, at 50 voters a day over the next 200 days (no money, no people but lots of time). Or you can contact all 10,000 tomorrow without any help by airing a great television and radio commercial. It will cost you a lot of money (no people, no time but money).

Effectiveness of your voter contact
Each type of voter contact can accomplish three things to varying degrees –

- persuade target voters,
- identify supporters
- turnout your vote

Voters need to know what your message is and they need to hear it many times for it to register with them. You must repeatedly communicate a persuasive message to people who will vote.

Persuade target voters
Everything you have done up to this point - all the research, setting the goal, targeting the audience and developing a persuasive message - has brought you to this point. Now you need to decide what is the easiest way for

you to communicate with this large group of people and convince them to vote for you. There is no point in having a great message if the voters do not know about it.

HOW?

People are often persuaded when they hear the same thing from many different sources. If they hear that you are a good candidate from a respected civic organization, meet the candidate going door to door, see some persuasive campaign literature, and read a favourable article in the newspaper, then they will more likely remember the candidate and more likely vote for that candidate.

Get out the vote

The "get out the vote" effort is often viewed as a separate phase of the campaign. In fact, it should be viewed as the final phase toward which everything else in the campaign builds. If you compare a political campaign to a business selling a product, in this case selling the candidate to the voters, then Election Day is the only day in which you can make the "sale".

Voter identification

It is important to know how you will identify supporters starting early in the campaign. You need to spend resources persuading your voters. However, if you only communicate with them, you are relying on them to go to the polls on their own. This can be a gamble that you need not take. You can increase your chances if you know who has been convinced and you have the ability to get them to the polls.

It is often possible to find out which candidate voters support just by asking them. Although are reluctant, most people generally like to be asked their opinion and are willing to tell you what they are thinking. Develop a simple "1-2-3" scale so that a confirmed supporter is labelled a "1," an undecided voter is a "2," and a supporter of an opponent is a "3." As your campaign communicates with voters, try to judge their level of support. You will want to spend most of your resources on number "2" voters in your target constituencies.

Types of voter contact activities

With all of these things in mind, it is important to ask the following questions as you consider the various types of voters' contact channels and strategies.

1. How much does it cost in time, money and people?
2. Do you know what voters are being reached?
3. Are they being persuaded?
4. Can you find out if they support your candidate and make sure that they vote for your candidate?

DEVELOPING A VOTER CONTACT PLAN

There are many access channels to voters and an analysis need to be done to determine the most effective channels to use. Your decision will be determined by several factors such as speed and cost. But the salient contact activities are as follows:

- Mail
- Door to door
- Phoning
- Visibility
- Endorsements
- Social events (such as Coffee morning etc)
- Friends of a friend
- Pre-set events
- Created events
- Earned media - the press
- Paid media - television, radio and newspaper advertisements
- Internet web pages
- Combining various methods

An Access Channel Strategy may be needed to determine the most effective channel to reach different categories of voters. This will be a combination of cost and performance potential of each channel.

CHAPTER EIGHT

HOW TO DETERMINE WHICH VOTER CONTACT METHODS TO USE

Choosing the correct access channels is vitally important as it will determine your ability to be persuasive to your target voters.

Not all access channels are effective in reaching all categories of voters. You must therefore choose the right channel for the right group of people.

Use the following chart to help determine which voter contact method your campaign will choose. It is important to be realistic.

No campaign should consider using all of the methods listed. This would just spread your resources too thin and guarantee that you did none of them well.

You will want to consider realistically what resources of time, money and people you will have available to you and how much each method will cost.

It is also important to pick various methods that, when combined, will accomplish all of the tasks - persuading voters, identifying supporters and turning out your vote.

Make a list of all the methods you have decided to use in your campaign and try to determine in hard numbers how much time, money and people you will need to accomplish your objective.

Voter contact task	Effectiveness			Resources		
	Persuade Voters	Identify Supporters	Turn-out Vote	Time	Money	People
Literature Drop	Yes	No	Yes	Yes		Yes
Literature Handouts	Maybe	No	Maybe			Yes
Mail	Yes	No	Yes		Yes	
Door to Door	Yes	Yes	No	Yes		Yes
Phoning	Maybe	Yes	Yes	Yes	Yes	Yes
Visibility	No	No	Yes	Yes	Yes	Yes
Endorsements	Yes	Maybe	Maybe	Yes		Yes
Coffees	Yes	Yes	No	Yes		Yes
Dear Friend	Yes	No	Yes	Yes		Yes

Voter contact task	Effectiveness			Resources		
	Persuade Voters	Identify Supporters	Turn-out Vote	Time	Money	People
Preset Events	Maybe	Maybe	No	Yes		Yes
Created Events	Maybe	No	Maybe	Yes	Yes	Yes
Press	Yes	No	Maybe	Yes		
Advertisements	Yes	No	Yes		Yes	
Web Pages	No	No	No			

Key features of a voter contact plan

From the tables above, you can see that there is a need to prioritise the most effective access channels to your target audience. Some things are essential to bear in mind when doing this.

CREATIVE CAMPAIGN LITERATURE

A set of clear and plain English (or any other domestic language) literature will be needed by the campaign. To produce a creative literature, the campaign need to focus on factors such as originality, ease of comprehension, visual appeal and correct use of colours. The style and tone should be consistent with your campaign branding.

SINGLE TOPIC

It is often advisable that in addition to a general introduction literature, the campaign should also create some single-issue literatures to address single topics of importance to the voters. Such focused publications will enable the candidate to articulate detailed policy positions in a way that demonstrates a good grasp of the issues facing the voters.

ACTION PHOTOS

There should be emphasis on using action photographs of the candidate rather than studio static images. A candidate seen as active plays well in the minds of the electorate.

So, pictures of the candidate in the public market, at bus stops, in the supermarket, on the street meeting ordinary people will play much better than banal studio images of a candidate that looks detached from the realities of ordinary citizen. Remember that in politics, perception is everything.

Also use images to soften the look of your campaign publications. Most voters will not have the time to read long essays that is not correctly completed by images. Images speaks louder than words.

HEADLINES

How stories are captioned is very important. In fact, research has shown that lots of people will only read the headline and form an opinion just based on that alone.

So, a campaign need excellent cation and headline writers that will perfectly encapsulate the essence of a story in a salient way.

BULLETED POINTS

Long prose does not play well in a campaign publication. Try to use bullet points to capture the gist of the story. It also looks better on the eyes.

BE SPECIFIC

Be specific on what you are trying to communicate and who you are communicating with. Every literature released by the campaign must have an intended audience within the voters' pool being targeted.

BREVITY

Any campaign literature that is more than a few pages long will not be read by most voters. There is need for detailed policy documents for the few anoraks to digest in full.

But for most voters that will be too much information. So, there is need to ensure mass produced literatures are as brief as possible.

STAY ON MESSAGE

Make sure all publications of the campaign accentuate the same message; which will be the essence of the campaign.

The message of the campaign must be repeated in all publications in one way or another. Repeated exposure to the same message makes it stick in people's minds.

CHAPTER NINE

MEDIA MANAGEMENT IN POLITICAL CAMPAIGN

The approach of a political campaign towards media management will be determined partly by the kind of person the candidate is. Candidates that are charismatic and controversial already can deploy strategies that allows them to get news-led free publicity while the more quieter candidates may have to rely on lot more paid publicity.

For instance, in the USA, President Trump spent the least of any candidate in modern US history on paid media publicity. Most of his media exposure were through News items due to his controversial nature and statements. So, he did not have to pay for exposure.

Although there is a downside to free publicity and that is the inability of the campaign to control the narrative. If the media decide to make mockery of a candidate (in ways that harms the campaign) for instance; then a lot of paid publicity may be required to counter this.

For example, in the 2017 presidential elections in Kenya; President Kenyatta got lots of free news-led publicity about his alleged drinking problem.

The media was awash with allegations and clips of him appearing drunk on several occasions at public events, even though this was denied by his media aids. This is an example of free publicity that can harm a campaign and need to be neutralised through paid publicity to correct any negative impression.

Also critical is the nature of the media landscape in the African country concerned. Some countries do not have free and fair media, some have media largely controlled and owned by politicians while others have semblance of free media. So, there cannot be a one size fits all media strategy for all of the continent. Jurisdictional peculiarities will need to be taken into account.

Some of the common tactics used by campaigns and political parties to manage the media during elections are:[3]

Dictate the agenda. Usually competing political parties or candidates prefer to fight a campaign on familiar terrain. One party may debate an election on the issue of, say,

---

[3] https://aceproject.org/ace-en/topics/me/mef/mef04/mef040c/mef04a

management of the economy. Another may focus on national security. The success of their campaign strategies depends on their abilities to spur media coverage of their chosen issues, and neglect those of the opposition. Journalists should be attentive to these intentions and provide balanced focus on each contender's issues as well as concerns of voters.

Use soft news to make parties and candidates appear voter-friendly. This tactic is as old as politics. Politicians shake hands, kiss babies, drink a pint of beer, go bowling – whatever is the culturally appropriate way to show that they are someone a voter would want to get to know as a friend or neighbour.

Voters generally know that these soft news opportunities are staged, yet the tactics are still successful in their intention. Soft news is also a means of avoiding issues that might be potentially damaging to a party or candidate platform. Journalists often face a dilemma, therefore. Soft news is not really proper news – however, media outlets competition by rival media outlets if they do not run it. This is one reason why election coverage can sometimes tend toward superficial and uninformative content.

Change the subject. This is closely related to the two previous points. In instances where events may damage a platform, parties and candidates will hastily seek to shift media focus elsewhere, such as the opposition's shortcomings, or a different manifesto pledge.

Incumbent parties are especially well placed to do this, as they can easily divert attention to official events or announcements.

Maintain media coverage. Notwithstanding the points mentioned above, party and candidate media managers generally work on the assumption that there is no such thing as bad publicity. There is an element of truth in this stance during elections. No one ever voted for a candidate they had not heard of.

Plant negative stories about the opposition. Attitudes toward negative political campaigning vary enormously depending on political culture. In most cases, however, verbal attacks on rival parties and candidates are considerably less effective than cleverly placed negative stories.

A journalist is therefore responsible, when confronted with negative stories, to ask the question: "who is telling me this – and what are their potential motives?"

Use of third-party PR techniques. This happens when a campaign sponsors an "expert" or a third party to write about an issue that supports the candidate's position without making it known he/she is speaking on behalf of the candidate or party.

The appearance of independence gives such opinion more credibility in the eyes of the voters than a simple campaign press release on the same issue.

The perception of unbiased opinion misleads the public into giving more weight to such views as it is coming from an "independent" person. At least that is what the public thinks.

Journalist organisations and governments in several countries in Africa have developed codes of conduct to guide their operations during political campaigns. Two of these codes of conduct from two different countries are referenced in Appendix Four of this book for information.

As can be seen, these codes of conduct reflect national judicial and operational peculiarities across the continent. But common to all of them are certain ethical themes which include:

- Accuracy

- Impartiality
- Honesty and resistance to corruption
- Avoiding the use of language or sentiments that promote violence or discrimination
- Correction of inaccurate factual reporting, and so on.

I have reproduced[4] two of these codes from Egypt and Tanzania as examples but most countries in Africa do have this code either through the unions and trade bodies or through government regulators.

I have taken time to explain the need to understand the operational framework for the media in your own country. This will inform how you manage the media during a campaign.

And if a code does not exist in your own country, you can follow the ethos of the

---

[4] In Appendix Four

International Federation of Journalist[5] as a template.

While the use of Social Media is on the rise in Africa, a political campaign cannot ignore the traditional media at all as many in the rural communities still rely on their radios to connect with the outside world.

Building a good relationship with Journalists and Editors become crucial in politics. As a campaign, your chief strategist should already have prepared scenario responses to the media based on what will come out about your candidate.

The *Message Boxing* exercise earlier discussed, should have flagged all the potential negative news that will come out about your candidate. Responses should have been considered for each negative news scenarios.

---

[5] http://www.ifj.org/about-ifj/ifj-code-of-principles/

The Use of Social Media

Africa is experiencing an explosion in social media usage as more and more countries roll out mobile 3G/4G technologies. With an overwhelmingly youthful population, many countries have seen an exponential increase in the use of social media. As evidenced during the 2016 presidential campaign in the USA; social media also attracts lots of fake news.

There are so many false and fake news these days it is difficult to know the truth from the untruth. People create news in the comfort of their own house and post them online easily. It is therefore essential for any political campaign to have a **dedicated Social Media Team**.

Our research has shown that many in Africa believe what they read online too readily. False news has led to many unrests and riots in several countries. A campaign therefore cannot afford to leave things to change or ignore the social media. There are many ways a campaign can leverage the social media to its benefit. Some of the key use of social media are:

For Branding and Message Push
Proper use of the social media can enable a campaign to craft social media strategies consistent with the messaging, platform, and objectives of the campaign.

The vision of the campaign can be reinforced through social media push on all platforms. Crafting high-impact, engaging posts can help to increase your visibility as a campaign. This will help the candidate to shape the conversation online and offline

For Constituency Relationship and Outreach
Social media can be used to expand the campaign's reach by rapidly building a robust following on social media. Building a community of constituents and providing an

open channel of communication with voters will become easier and cheaper. This will allow a direct access to voters, thus allowing the campaign to dictate the narrative and put its own spin of the news.

For Managing Supporters and Getting the Vote Out

Social media helps the campaign to avoid the need and expense to set up its own voter contact applications and technical infrastructure. Using existing platforms such as Facebook and Twitter, the campaign will be able to provide a central hub for supporters, volunteers, staff members, and constituents to learn about the latest events, rallies, messages, and fundraisers.

Building a community of constituents and providing an open channel of communication with voters is a major benefit of the Social Media.

Coordinating all efforts to get out the votes on election day will also become easier and more effective.

For Fundraising
With Social Media, promoting campaign events, initiating contact with potential donors, driving traffic to donation websites, and directly soliciting contributions from followers will become easier.

It also allows you to generate excitement and increase contributions by planning and managing innovative online fundraising initiatives and events.

For Crisis and Reputation Management
Ability to reach out and communicate directly with potential voters without the filtering of journalists can be a powerful tool for a campaign to correct wrong assumptions and manage any crisis in the campaign.

Also, patrolling social media for mentions of you and your campaign becomes possible and easier as part of your reputation monitoring exercise. This allows the campaign to identify potentially damaging messaging across social media and working in concert with your strategists to craft appropriate, immediate and high-impact responses.

Using social media to propel positive messaging about you and your campaign to the forefront of search engines.

With all these benefits, it is therefore important for the candidates to create time to learn and know how social media works. If the candidate is trained and skilled enough, he/she should be encouraged to put out messages directly and personally on social media from time to time.

There is an added excitement in the voters knowing that the candidate is writing his own twitter postings than the media department doing the same.

Consistency is also important. The candidate must be consistent in the use of Social Media in order to build and strengthen support base and make Social Media platforms believable channels of receiving communication by the supporters.

Building a coalition and outreach to civic organisations
This is an important aspect of building credibility for the candidate. Voters tend to believe more statements by people or organisations perceived to be independent of the campaign.

So, civic organisations can be of value in many ways including the following:
- Endorsement
- Mobilize membership
- Press events

- Research
- Public events
- Outreach

Working with your party

Coordination of campaign activities with the party is vital. Some of the things to have in mind are:

- Message and information
- Material design
- National materials
- Press
- Visits
- Endorsements

It is advisable for the candidate to be in charge of his/her own campaign. Political parties are notorious for messing things up for candidates.

Remember; as a candidate, you can only fully trust your own team and not necessarily those in the party HQ who may have allegiances to the other candidates you defeated at the primaries. But the parties will be crucial in managing volunteers and supporters. Hence a good relationship with the party is strongly advocated.

Post-Election Review

Finally, win or lose, a post-election review with the key campaign team is advisable. This will allow you to learn needed lessons for future campaigns. As a politician whether elector or not; there is always another campaign to fight in the future. So, no lessons learnt is ever wasted.

And if you win an election, keep a few of your campaign inner team close as they may be needed to keep you on message while in office to ensure voters expectations are met and managed. Your next election will depend on how closely matched your campaign promises and your deliverables in office are.

Wishing you all the best in the campaign ahead.

APPENDIX ONE

ELEMENTS OF A CAMPAIGN PLAN

In short, a campaign plan defines what is to be done, when it should be done, who should be doing it, and what resources will be needed to complete the job.

A solid campaign plan lays out the contextual information of each constituency, voter information analysis, campaign strategy and tactics, staffing and resource requirements.

Therefore, the major elements of a campaign plan should include most of the following:

- A **constituency by constituency analysis** including geographic, social, economic, and demographic information on the constituencies and a breakdown of the political implications of that information.

- **Electoral research** focused on each constituency's voting history, voter turnout and other voting trends if available. Electoral research also helps a campaign estimate the ultimate question in a campaign: *"How many votes do we need to win?"*

- **Candidate and opposition profiles** focus on the major personal, political, and policy characteristics associated with all candidates in the race.

- In the **campaign message** a candidate answers the question; *"Why am I running?"* Also, the campaign message provides reasons to support a candidate. For instance, if a supporter is asked in a line at the Bank, *"I see you are wearing a X candidate T Shirt.*

Why are you supporting him?"; the supporter's response is the campaign message: "I'm voting for X-Ticket because. . . . . . ."

- **Budget and fund-raising plans** are separate, but related, activities. Creating a budget informs the campaign about how much money it needs to raise and how it will be spent (for example, for paid media, fund-raisers, postage for mailings, and so on). The fund-raising plan tells the campaign how the funds specified in the budget will be raised; it projects not only an amount that will be raised and the sources from which it will likely be raised, but more importantly the specific strategies the campaign will use to raise the money.

- A **volunteer recruitment and volunteer use plan** focuses on how to identify and recruit volunteers, how to use them most efficiently and effectively when they show up, and how to keep them happy and coming back to volunteer again.

- A **paid media plan** centres on the strategic decisions that involve all paid communications or advertisements (for example, direct mail literature, newspaper, TV, or radio ads, and billboards) and all campaign collateral materials (for example, signs, campaign buttons, bumper stickers, and other literature). The paid media plan also will include information on the planned timing of ads, when literature will be distributed, and so on.

- An **earned media plan** designs activities geared toward generating enough media interest in the campaign so the campaign's events are covered as a news story. The earned media plan needs to be specific and cover activities such as interviews with journalists, and speeches the candidate will give, and candidate forums or debates that are likely to be covered by the news media.

- A **get-out-the-vote plan** informs the campaign on how voters who have been identified as supporters will be mobilized on Election Day; plus an incentives necessary to make this happen.

- The **campaign calendar** brings all the different elements of the plan together in chronological order. Since all campaigns work with the same time constraints—there are only a certain number of days until Election Day— proper planning through the use of a campaign calendar helps ensure that time-consuming activities are completed at the appropriate time by detailing the dates by which all campaign activities must be performed.

APPENDIX TWO

CRAFTING THE CAMPAIGN MESSAGE

Remember, campaigns are about giving voters a choice, and it is the campaign's purpose to show voters why their candidate should be the preferred choice.

Along with opposition and candidate research, some campaigns conduct a SWOT (Strengths, Weaknesses, Opportunities, Threats) analysis of the candidates, the context, and the issues.

Identifying positives and negatives about each candidate continues to help the people running the campaign identify potential comparisons that may be useful to the candidate throughout the campaign.

A related device commonly used when developing a campaign message and identifying contrasts between candidates is a message box. Similar to a SWOT analysis, a message box identifies strengths and weaknesses of each candidate.

However, it goes a step further and helps campaign personnel identify contrasts that will give their candidate an advantage with voters. In the message box, a candidate tries to define himself, define his opponent(s), and define the issues in the campaign by dividing strengths and weaknesses into the quadrants of the box.

This helps the campaign to identify what each candidate is likely to try to say during the campaign (see Box sample below). In this way, a campaign can be positioned relative to its opponent(s), and be better able to offer voters choices that favour the candidate

OUTLINE OF A CAMPAIGN MESSAGE BOX

Outline of a Campaign Message Box	
Us on Us What we want to say about our candidate and our campaign	**Us on Them** What we want to say about the opponent and the campaign
Them on Us What our campaign anticipates the opponent will say about our candidates and our campaign	**Them on Them** What our campaign anticipates the opponent will say about himself candidate and his campaign

Campaign Theme v Campaign Message
Closely related to the campaign message is the **campaign theme**. The theme differs from the message in that the theme is what the campaign is about, whereas the message tells

potential voters why the candidate is the best choice rather than the opponent.

Incumbents running for re-election may employ a theme that encourages voters to *"stay the course"* or maintain the status quo. Many themes are used again and again, and have been utilised in campaigns over many years.

For instance, in his 1864 re-election campaign in the USA, President Abraham Lincoln said, *"Don't change horses in the middle of the stream";* many incumbent candidates use this same theme today, including George W. Bush in his 2004 US re-election bid. A similar approach of continuity was taken by President Kenyatta in his 2017 re-election bid in Kenya.

In contrast, challenger candidates may use a theme focusing on "change" for their campaign to try to urge potential voters to fire the incumbent. This change theme was used successfully by the Buhari presidential campaign in Nigeria's 2015 elections. **Messages stem from the theme, and are usually more specific statements that are tied to issues in the campaign.**

Please note that I am not saying that a campaign message begins and ends with research into each constituency; the electorate, or the opponent. Rather, a campaign message begins with what the candidates want to do once elected to office.

A candidate's campaign is about his vision for the future and his policy ideas. To be successful, a candidate must have an idea of where he wants to go once elected and what he wants to do for the voters.

The research that is conducted vitally helps to refine those ideas and create contrasts between the candidate and the opponent(s), illustrating the choices voters have between the candidates.

APPENDIX THREE

SAMPLE SEQUENCE OF ACTIONS AND NEXT STEPS

As we conclude this book, the key question now is; what are the next steps to put things into action and launch a new political campaign. The structure of a campaign will largely depend on the nature of the office the candidate is running for. So, there is no one rigid structure for every campaign.

For instance, a structure set up for a national Presidential campaign will be an overkill for a local government election campaign. So, the structure will need to be proportionate to the office being sought by the candidate.

But as a general rule the following are some possible next steps that can be tweaked to fit any campaign. It will of course have to be scaled up or down to suit each campaign.

1) Establish an Advisory Group (Up to Seven to Ten People Maximum)

2) Candidate to establish a "Political Fund" to which well-wishers and foot soldiers can begin to contribute into.

3) Engage the services of a political Strategist.

4) Task Advisory Group with producing a Campaign Strategy working with the strategist.

5) Provide Initial Campaign Funding

6) Initial Campaign Strategy Produced & Ready

7) Establish the top three levels of the Campaign Organization Structure as suggested below.

8) Choose and Instruct a Marketing/Research Firm with the help of the strategist.

9) Choose and Instruct a PR/Media Firm working with the strategist.

10) First Quarterly Review of Campaign Strategy and a continuous review after.

Sample Campaign Organization Structure

Campaign Organisation Structure

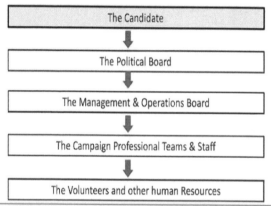

1. The **Political Board** will consist of the **Candidate, 4 senior** & experienced political colleagues as well as the **Chair and the Vice Chair** of the Management & Operations Board. **This will be the Final Decision making Body for the campaign, and <u>made of 7 Members in total.</u>**

2. **The Management & Operations Board** runs the Campaign on a **day to day basis.** They also manage all budgets, consultants; the media, suppliers as well as manage the Campaign staff and Volunteers.

Campaign Budget / Funding

Campaign Budget/Funding tends to be classed into two categories:

- Technical & Operational Budget
- Political Activities Budget

Technical & Operational Budget

This budget can be fully assessed, after all the data/figures has been collected.

This Budget consists of:

- Running cost of campaign office including staffing
- Cost of Consultants and external services procured
- Cost of Logistics for constituency-wide campaign, including transportation; hire charges for venues etc.
- Cost of Adverts, promos, flyers, etc

This budget needs regular review to keep it relevant to developments in the campaign and market inflationary pressures.

More data is needed to produce a viable budget. This will be the responsibility of the initial working group of the campaign.

An initial outline cost should be produced as part of the initial Campaign Strategy. Some initial financial outlay is however needed to kick-start the process as noted below.

ESSENTIAL CAMPAIGN STAFF

– Campaign Director

– Chief Strategist

– Communications Director (Reports to the Chief Strategist)

– Legal & Field Director (Reports to the Chief Strategist)

--Volunteer coordinator

– Fundraiser & Campaign Treasurer

– Campaign Administrator & Scheduler

– Policy Researcher

MINIMUM INFRASTRUCTURE STARTUP REQUIREMENTS

As a start; the following need to be provided by the Candidate or her supporters:

- A furnished and equipped office space for the use of the Campaign.

- Employment of an Office Administrator that will facilitate liaison amongst advisory group members. This role must be willing to travel constituency-wide.

- A politically astute and media savvy PA need to be appointed for the Candidate soonest.

  This person will travel everywhere with the Candidate to enforce Campaign Strategic standards and procedures and assist the Candidate to "Stay on Message".

- A couple of Vehicles and drivers need to be made available for the use of the Campaign.

- A couple of mobile phone lines dedicated for the campaign.

- An initial sum made available for Operational expenditures, running costs etc. This will be overall managed by the Campaign Director (When appointed).

Political Activities Budget

Unlike the Technical and Operations budget; this Budget can never be estimated in full in advance.

This is the budget for political donations and gifts given by the candidate for political reasons. This will usually be at the discretion of the candidate.

It is impossible to estimate the total budget for this in advance. This budget is controlled only by the Candidate, based on his/her financial capabilities. Funds for voter incentives activities come under this budgetary provision.

MAKING IT HAPPEN – Implementation Phases & Milestones.

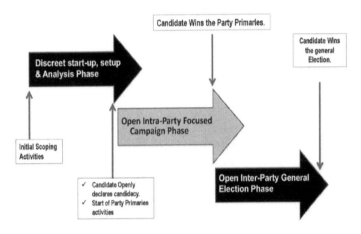

Sample implementation sequence

Finally

An initial meeting between the Candidate and possible members of the initial Advisory Group need to take place soonest. Everything else will be clearer after this meeting.

APPENDIX FOUR

SAMPLE CODES OF CONDUCT FOR JOURNALISTS DURING ELECTION CAMPAIGNS FROM DIFFERENT AFRICAN COUNTRIES

(EGYPT) Professional Code of Ethics for Media Coverage of General Elections[6]

First: GENERAL PRINCIPLES

(1) Media personnel believe that media coverage of electoral campaigns aims at corroborating all the rights enshrined in the Universal Declaration of Human Rights, the International Covenant for

---

[6] This code of ethics was prepared by Salah Essa – Editor in chief of Cairo newspaper. The Code of Ethics reached this final draft after a series of meetings between Salah Essa, CIHRS and a number of Egyptian Prominent Journalist with different backgrounds and ideologies, for more information look: "What role for the media in covering general elections, manual for domestic and international practices", Giovanna Mayola and Sobhy Essaila, Cairo Institute for Human Rights Studies, 2010

Civil and Political Rights; particularly provisions of direct relevance to general elections, including the first paragraph of article XXI of the Charter, which guarantees the right of every individual to participate in the management of public affairs of his/her country, either directly or through freely elected representatives; and the third paragraph of the same article, which provides that the will of the people is the source of government authority, and that the people will express this will in periodic and impartial elections, performed on secret ballot basis, on an equal footing for all, or according to any similar procedure ensuring freedom of voting.

This meaning is also stipulated in the first paragraph of Article 25 of the International Covenant for Civil and Political Rights, which recognizes the right of every citizen in the conduct of public affairs, either directly or through freely chosen representatives, and the second paragraph of the same article, which guarantees to every citizen to vote and be elected in genuine periodic elections on the basis of equal suffrage and that the elections shall be held by secret ballot, guaranteeing the free expression of the will of the electors.

(2) Media personnel believe that their role in the media coverage of election campaigns is not merely a commitment to provisions of Article 19 of the Universal Declaration of Human Rights, regarding the right of everyone to receive and impart information and ideas through any media, as an imperative right and duty; to raise public opinion awareness and interest through general elections, as a right and duty ; to stimulate citizens to participate in elections, through voting and nomination and; to believe that they are the public opinion vehicle to monitor the integrity and transparency of the electoral process.

"(3) Media personnel cling tight, in media coverage of the general elections, to all the rights guaranteed by the public law, the Press Law, the Law on the Exercise of Political Rights, and the Presidential Election Law, the Press Code of Honour, and– as well – they abide by all the duties imposed on them by these laws and conventions, according to details provided for in this Declaration.

(4) Mass media shall make a clear distinction between advertising and editing on the one hand, and news and opinion on the other, with respect to coverage of election campaigns. They may not publish electoral advertising material under the guise of an editorial, even if not directly related to the elections. Owners of the newspapers and media may not receive, directly or indirectly, any financial support from political parties and figures engaging in election campaigns, during the entire period between the nomination and the announcement of final results of elections, including the publication of commercials for economic ventures or companies in which candidates are shareholders.

(5) Newspapers of all kinds shall be committed, when releasing the results of public opinion polls on voter attitudes vis-à-vis candidates, to highlight more clearly in their headlines and in the body of their reports, the size of the sample having participated in the poll and the authority having conducted it, and the date of the poll.

They shall not publish or broadcast these findings in such a way as to suggest that it was administered to the overall electorate called upon to cast their ballots; and the entity preparing the survey or the questionnaire should be an independent, specialized, and non-partisan legal person.

(6) National newspapers, private and independent mass media shall, in their published material on the election contest, be committed to absolute neutrality between all parties and candidates competing in these elections, provide them equal opportunities, including personal information and platforms, and shall not make any distinction between candidates in terms of photographs, headlines or any means of highlighting, or in the prices of advertisement.

They may not - outside this scope- administer any interviews with one of the candidates, either immediately prior to or during the election campaign, even if the elections were not the subject of such interviews.

(7) Partisan newspapers shall be exempted from commitment to the text of the previous article. In the event any independent information medium decides to take sides with any of the candidates or parties, it must clearly indicate such whenever required. Neither national newspapers, nor TV channels and radio stations owned by the Radio and Television Union, shall enjoy this exemption.

They shall abide by provisions of Article 55 of the Law on Regulation of the Press, and as such, shall preserve their impartiality and independence from the Executive Estate and from all the political parties, and shall be committed to neutrality among all" "contenders."

(8) In case the independent information medium decides to take sides with any of the contending nominees or parties, it shall be under an obligation to clearly refer to such whenever necessary. In the event it publishes free advertisements, platforms, or editorial material in support of this candidacy, it shall be under an

obligation to refer to itself as the supporting entity.

(9) Impartiality of any information medium to any of the candidates or parties running in the elections does not give this medium the right to launch smearing campaigns against, or to distort, slander, defame, or politically undermine any of the contenders.

In all cases, all mass media shall undertake to preserve the rights established in the professional codes of conduct and public law in dealing with their contenders and antagonists, in terms of protection against slander, safeguarding the right to privacy, and focusing the disputes within an objective political context.

(10) All mass media shall refrain from publishing or broadcasting any electoral paid advertisements in favour of any candidates 48 hours prior to the scheduled date for the elections. They shall also abstain from administering any opinion polls or publishing results thereof regarding the electors' position vis-à-vis the candidates.

This provision shall not include all material related to elections, which fall beyond the scope of electoral paid advertisements for candidates."

Second: RIGHTS

"(1) Any journalist/reporter assigned to cover the general elections shall have the right to obtain copies of all the laws, resolutions, instructions, data, and reports about the electoral process and its development from the entity governing the electoral process as soon as they are proclaimed, since the beginning of nomination and until the announcement of the results. The competent administrative authority or the media which employs the journalist shall, as appropriate, provide him/her with the necessary material to facilitate the performance of his/her task in the requisite professional competence and in a timely manner; without discrimination between a newspaper and another.

(2) The employing authority shall provide the journalist/reporter with solid evidence and documents required for the performance of

his/her task, and to obtain the required authorizations from the authorities concerned, for the journalist/reporter and his/her assistant staff including photographers and others. The employing authority shall provide the journalist with a uniform easily recognizable from a distance, so that he/she may not be subject to any constraints or injury during the performance of his/her professional duty. The employing authority shall coordinate with the competent administrative bodies to ensure the security of the journalist/reporter. Information authorities shall act in concert to obtain administrative decisions from the competent authority which regulates the work of journalists/reporters so that they will not be subjected to any arbitrary interference with the performance of their mission.

(3) Any journalist/reporter shall be entitled to attend press conferences convened by the candidates, to enter into electoral headquarters of all the candidates and the outer zone of the electoral committees of either general or subsidiary elections, and to enter the committee during the voting process. He/she shall have the

right to attend the counting of the votes with the representatives of candidates. However, no more than three journalists/reporters shall be present simultaneously within the subsidiary election committee during the voting process, in addition to the sufficient number of assistance.

(4) The employer shall provide the journalist/reporter with the means of communication and transportation that would enable him/her to follow-up to elections and to timely send reports to the medium he/she is employed with.

(5) Journalists and media officers shall adhere to their right provided for in Article 12 of the Law on the Regulation of the Press No. 96 for the year 1996, which stipulates that anyone having insulted or abused a journalist because of his/her work shall be liable to the penalties prescribed for insulting or abusing a civil servant, in accordance with articles 133, 136 or 173/1 of the Penal Code as the case may be. The medium shall report any insult or affront of this kind as soon as it occurs.

Third: DUTIES

(1) Any journalist running for elections may not exercise the duties of his/her profession as of the beginning of the nomination process until the announcement of the results of the elections. Anyone working in the audio or visual press may not exercise his/her functions during that period, even if the material he/she writes or presents is not directly related to the electoral process. This shall not forfeit other rights he/she possesses as a candidate, and he/she should be treated on an equal footing with other candidates without any prejudices.

(2) Any journalist/reporter may not cover the elections in the constituency where his/her native origin is located, or where his/her name is registered in the electoral roasters.

(3) Any journalist/reporter covering the elections may not work in the media team of any party or candidate running in the elections, with the exception of journalists/reporters working for partisan newspapers.

(4) Any journalist/reporter may not work to attract electoral paid advertisements, either directly or indirectly.

(5) Any journalist/reporter covering the elections shall be committed to professionalism in drafting and editing reports on the electoral process, in terms of accuracy and documentation of information, the reference of words and deeds to well-known sources whenever available and possible. He/she shall also be committed to refrain from publishing incomplete or abridged news or reports, or deliberately conceal aspects of the truth or facts from the readers.

(6) Any journalist/reporter shall be committed to disclose all forms of deviance from the laws regulating the electoral process, in such a way as to affect the integrity thereof or inaccurately express the will of the voters, including:

a) Poor organization of the electoral process, in terms of lack of logistical preparedness to guarantee their smoothness; including: inaccurate electoral roasters, delaying the opening of election committees, spoiling of the phosphoric ink, or the absence of glass boxes, etc...

b) The use of in kind or financial bribes to buy votes out.

c) The use of slogans and rumours of a religious or sectarian nature in electoral campaigns, either in a declared or undeclared manner, in order either to attract or vend off voters.

d) Exposure of the private life of any of the candidates, except what is related to the public post of the candidate; or liable and slander."

e) The use of government facilities, or the resources of administrative bodies or municipalities, in advertising for any of the candidates, or facilitation of the transfer of his/her supporters."

f) The distribution of government services through one of the candidates."

g) Hindering voters', candidates, their delegates, and election monitors from civil society organizations access to the polls, and preventing them from entering therein."

h) Voters casting their ballots in public."

i) Expelling representatives of candidates from voting or counting committees, or placing fabricated obstacles to prevent them from fulfilling their mission."

j) The use of any form of physical or verbal violence against the supporters of rival candidates, candidates, their delegates, or election monitors from civil society organizations."

k) Excessively spending on electoral campaigns in such a way as to suggest that money is used to influence the will of the voters, or that it involves manifest violations of resolutions and laws governing expenditure on electoral advertisements."

(TANZANIA MAINLAND) MEDIA CODE OF CONDUCT FOR ELECTION REPORTING 2010

Preamble

We, practitioners and other stakeholders in the media industry:

Recognizing the significance of the forthcoming General Election;

Guided by the desire to ensure the success of this democratic process; and

Determined to ensure that voters make an informed choice;

HEREBY agree on and adopt a Code of Conduct for covering the Elections as follows:

1. Objectivity

(i) Journalists should provide fair, balanced and impartial reporting by giving equitable space and airtime to all sides of an issue and to give an aggrieved party and the complainant the right to reply.

(ii) Notwithstanding the foregoing, all journalists who are contesting political positions should stop or resign from practising journalism until the nomination or election process is completed.

(iii) Journalists should refrain from giving special favour to their colleagues who are contesting in the election.

2. Truth

(i) Journalists covering elections must seek the truth and report it precisely and soberly.

(ii) Media houses should do the utmost to correct promptly any published or aired information that is found to be inaccurate.

3. Response to the needs of voters

Journalists must provide the electorate with information and civic education in a form easily understood, to enable them to make informed choices.

4. Encouraging Free Speech

The media should encourage the public to express their opinion and views and should give them opportunities to do so.

5. Confidence Sources

Journalists should observe professional ethics regarding the sources of information obtained in confidence, but they should not use such information as an excuse to propagate their personal opinion.

6. Hate Speech and Incitement

When reporting the opinions of those who do advocate discrimination or violence on any grounds, including race, gender, language, religion, political or other opinions, and national or social origins, journalists should do the utmost to put such views in a clear context and to report the opinions of those against whom such sentiments are directed.

7. Promote Democratic Values

The media should promote democratic values such as the rule of law, accountability, good governance and political tolerance.

8. Media House Obligation

Media Houses and owners have an obligation to:
(i) Ensure impartial, fair and balanced coverage of elections and give equitable access to all

candidates and political parties because it is in the national and people's interest to do so;

(ii) Promote unity, peace, and stability.

(iii) Commit themselves to contribute towards the achievement of free and fair elections by developing the capacity of their respective media institutions and refraining from interfering in editorial independence.

9. Investigate issues

Journalists should have the responsibility to investigate and expose issues and practices pertaining to elections in order to facilitate fair play and level the socio-political playing ground.

10. Advertorials

Media houses should identify and charge equal rates to advertorials from all political parties but desist from publishing or airing advertorials, commentaries and columns that seek to create hatred and endanger national peace and security.

11. Media and the Election Acts

Media, like all other stakeholders in the election process, must strictly adhere to the Election Act and understand clearly the Elections Expenses

Act and regulations, and expose practices that violate it.

12. Media and Civil Society

The media should work in partnership with civil society in providing civic and voter education, training as well as monitoring and evaluating the entire electoral process.

13. Professional offences

Journalists shall regard the following as professional offences:

- Plagiarism
- Malicious misrepresentation
- Slander, libel or unfounded accusations
- Acceptance of a bribe in any form in consideration of either publication or suppression.

14. Opinion Polls

Media Houses should take care in reporting the findings of opinion polls. Any report should include the following information:

a) who commissioned and carried out the poll and when

b) how many people were interviewed

c) where and how they were interviewed

d) the margin of error

15. Media and Marginalised Groups

i. Journalists should promote the participation of the marginalized, including women, the disabled and the youth to take part in political leadership, they should also refrain from coverage that is biased, reinforcing existing prejudices against such groups.

ii. Media should encourage the above group to contest, irrespective of their political affiliation, by raising public awareness of their importance in public life, and by rebuking all moves aimed at suppressing them. Journalists should also show the public

OTHER BOOKS BY DR CHARLES OMOLE

Some of Dr Omole's key publications are:

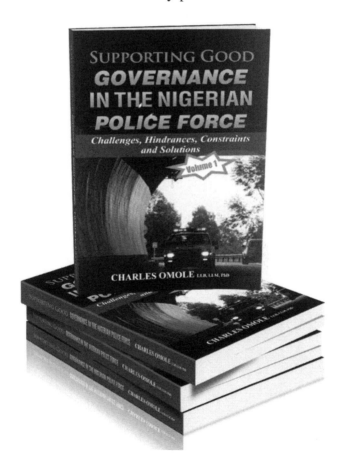

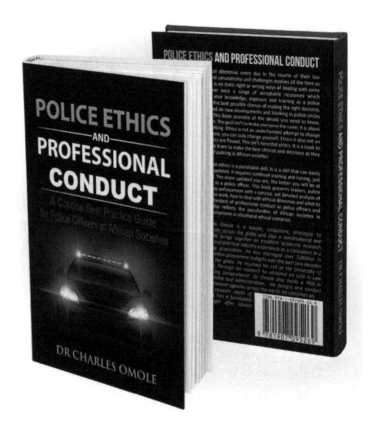

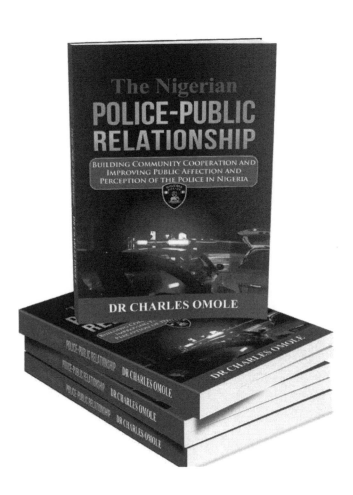

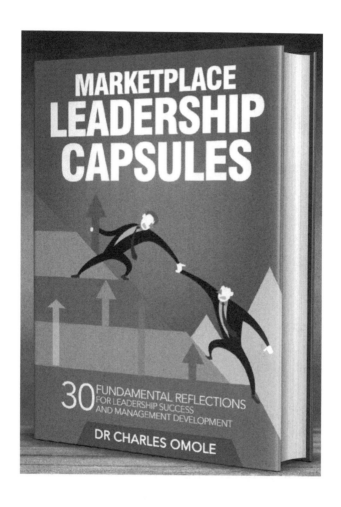

Dr. CHARLES OMOLE can be reached on:

Info@Prodelglobalservices.com
Or
Charlesomole@gmail.com

NOTES

NOTES

Printed in Poland
by Amazon Fulfillment
Poland Sp. z o.o., Wrocław

62988619R00103